About the Author

Peter Denison was commissioned from the RMA, Sandhurst, into an infantry regiment. He resigned his commission in the rank of Captain in order to commence training as a probation officer, remaining in the Probation Service for thirty-seven years. After becoming a Christian in 1974, he was involved in various Christian rehabilitation offender related charities, including Probation Service Christian Fellowship (National Chairman), Prison Fellowship (South East England Co-ordinator) and Stepping Stones Trust (SST Chairman for twenty-eight years) – receiving an OBE for his work in SST. He has a passionate interest in seeing the Lord working in the lives of prisoners.

Freedom in Christ

Peter Denison

Freedom in Christ

Olympia Publishers
London

www.olympiapublishers.com
OLYMPIA PAPERBACK EDITION

Copyright © Peter Denison 2022

The right of Peter Denison to be identified as author of
this work has been asserted in accordance with sections 77 and 78 of
the Copyright, Designs and Patents Act 1988.

All Rights Reserved

No reproduction, copy or transmission of this publication
may be made without written permission.
No paragraph of this publication may be reproduced,
copied or transmitted save with the written permission of the publisher,
or in accordance with the provisions
of the Copyright Act 1956 (as amended).

Any person who commits any unauthorised act in relation to
this publication may be liable to criminal
prosecution and civil claims for damage.

A CIP catalogue record for this title is
available from the British Library.

ISBN: 978-1-80074-378-6

This is a work of creative nonfiction. The events are portrayed to the best of the author's memory. While all the stories in this book are true, some names and identifying details have been changed to protect the privacy of the people involved.

First Published in 2022

Olympia Publishers
Tallis House
2 Tallis Street
London
EC4Y 0AB

Printed in Great Britain

Acknowledgements

My thanks to Bob Kimmerling, a former CEO of Stepping Stones Trust, who sensitively compiled for this book the testimonies by ex-prisoners.

Contents

Chapter 1 The Gospel – proclaiming freedom for prisoners 11

Chapter 2 The Gospel – conveyed by God using the principle of minimum force 16

How the Gospel influenced two national leaders 21

Chapter 3 King George VI – The Earth is the Lord's 21

Chapter 4 Donald Trump – the day of small things? 25

How the gospel affected some sex offenders Chapter 5 Setting up a Sex Offender Hostel 29

Chapter 6 A poem advocating compassion for those on 'the margins of society.' 34

Chapter 7 Introduction to Ex-Prisoners Testimonies 35

Chapter 8 A Sex Offender's Testimony 37

How the Gospel effected 'ordinary' offenders

Chapter 9 Alex 39

Chapter 10 Brian 42

Chapter 11 Colin 44

Chapter 12 Dennis 49

Chapter 13 Ernest 55

Chapter 14 Fred 61

Conclusion 67

Chapter 1
The Gospel – proclaiming freedom for prisoners

1. <u>Introduction</u>. My first book, *Freedom for Prisoners,* published by Olympia Publishers, described how the Lord impacted the lives of prisoners. The book mainly concentrated on talks I gave to prisoners and included some Christian counselling; its sequel, *Freedom in Christ,* explores the gospel, especially in regards to its effect on the lives of Christian ex-prisoners, as told by the ex-prisoners themselves.

2. <u>The gospel</u>. The main characteristic of the gospel is that Jesus Christ is both Lord and Saviour. It demands an obedient response to all that God has done for humanity, in particular, faith in Christ, repentance from sin, baptism and becoming like Christ through discipleship. Mark 1:14, *'Jesus went into Galilee, proclaiming the good news of God. "The time has come," he said, "The kingdom of God is near. Repent and believe the good news."'*[1] The gospel is the core of Jesus' teaching.

3. The gospel produces freedom in Christ – Galatians 5:1, *'It is for freedom that Christ has set us free. Stand firm, then, and do not let yourselves be burdened again by a yoke*

---

[1] All scripture quotations in this book (unless otherwise stated) are taken from the *life Application Bible (New International Version),* Kingsway Publications, Eastbourne, 1988.

of slavery.' This statement by Paul sums up his letter to the Galatian churches, which were founded by him during his first missionary journey. Many of the converts came from a Jewish background, and felt constrained to follow the strict Jewish laws. Paul was encouraging them to put off this 'yoke of slavery' in regards to these laws and instead concentrate on their new found faith and freedom in Christ.

4. Christ came to remove many different 'yokes of slavery.' The main one being our slavery to sin resulting in separation from God, which is spiritual death. At 'new birth' God decrees that our sins are forgiven and we are reconciled to God, enabling us to enter into a meaningful relationship with Christ. Having been freed from the penalty of sin, we are no longer under a yoke of slavery to sin. This does not mean that we will no longer sin but that we are not in slavery to our sin loving nature.

5. Christ provides freedom from the fear of death. The New Testament Church experienced persecution – most of the apostles becoming martyrs. Persecution has become a longstanding feature of the Christian Church. The removal of the fear of death does not mean that we expect God to remove persecution, or the prospect of death, but rather that in recognizing our natural weakness, we are given God's strength and He will be with us, to enable us to live victoriously. Many of our smaller trials can be times of joy, when we can profit by adopting a positive attitude because in these times of learning we develop perseverance and patience. This prepares us for the subsequent greater trials that we will almost inevitably have to face.

6. Owing to the Covid pandemic there is a new awakening to the fragility of life. The very fact that death is

so feared, to some extent bears witness of the truth of a saying by the wise King Solomon, who wrote, '*He* (God) *has made everything beautiful in its time. He has also set eternity in the hearts of men; yet they cannot fathom what God has done from beginning to end.*' (Ecclesiastes 3:11). In other words, we don't want to die because the Creator God has given us a deep desire to live forever. Solomon also observed that humanity '*cannot recognize what God has done.*' No doubt the thinking of Solomon was influenced by his father, King David, who made the same point rather more bluntly when he wrote, '*The fool says in his heart, "There is no God"* (Psalm 14:1).

7. Christ took on our human nature so that in His death and resurrection, He could destroy Satan's power over death, thus delivering those who lived in fear of death. The writer of Hebrews described it this way, to '*free those who all their lives were held in slavery by their fear of death.*' (Hebrews 2:15)

8. Christ rescues us from this present evil age. This does not mean He takes us out of this world but rather loosens the world's attractions so that we are no longer enslaved to the desire for wealth, immorality, status, harmful addictive habits, which all operate under the guiding principles of selfishness and pride. As Christians, with eternity in our hearts, we come to realize that there is so much more available in life than these transitionary pleasures, as we accept in faith the future prospect of eternal life in Christ.

9. Jesus said, "*If you hold to my teaching, you are really my disciples. Then you will know the truth, and the truth will set you free*" (John 8:31-32). Jesus is the source

of all truth, so everything He says is true. During a discussion He had with a Samaritan woman about worship, He told the woman, *"True worshippers will worship the Father in spirit and truth, for they are the kind of worshippers the Father seeks"* (John 4:23). The purpose in going to church should be to worship God in 'spirit and truth,' anything short of that can be 'going through the motions' with the wrong attitude. Attending church is not just a Sunday ritual but an important opportunity, with other believers, to glorify God. If we are to experience Christ's freedom, we need to examine our habitual routines to check whether we really want to glorify God, or are just following traditional habits, without any real heart for God.

10. John 8:36, *"So if the Son sets you free, you will be free indeed."* Christ did not free us to enable us to do whatever we want, as this would only lead us back into a slavery to our selfish desires. Instead, we must do what we used to find hard – to live unselfishly. Pride can so easily creep into our attitude so that we take on one of our society's aims, which is visibility, where the main intention is to impress others. Our good deeds should be motivated by Christ's love and hidden from others. If they are deliberately visible to others, Christ says that we have 'our reward' there and then – in the approval of the world. As Christians we should become more aware of the unseen, eternal world to where we are heading.

11. How do we experience this freedom? What are the mechanics to enable this to work, bearing in mind we are considering things of the Spirit? When God created humanity, He gave each of us a body, soul and spirit. The spirit was given so that with it we could communicate with

God, who is Spirit. *'Now the Lord is the Spirit, and where the Spirit of the Lord is, there is freedom'* (2 Corinthians 3:17). At new birth our spirit is awakened out of a comatose existence and suddenly finds a natural affinity with the Holy Spirit, so through this freedom in Christ we are no longer struggling to find God, who is manifested in our spirit. The nearest analogy is a tone-deaf person suddenly receiving a new appreciation of music. God's presence fills our heart with wonder, joy, love and thanksgiving. We are amazed that God has made Himself known to us. For a fuller understanding about becoming a Christian, read my book *Freedom for Prisoners,* chapter 15, entitled, 'How to become a Christian.'

Chapter 2
The Gospel – conveyed by God using the principle of minimum force

1. Back in 1964, after being commissioned from the Royal Military Academy, Sandhurst, my first posting as a subaltern was in Malta where, at the time, our regiment was expecting civil unrest, so we were training to combat potential crowd disturbances. One of the key internal security training principles was the 'use of minimum force' for this task. This involved starting with the least oppressive measure to control a rioting crowd, but if this failed, progressively using stronger measures of control. After laying out a barbed wire fence (as a protection for my platoon), we would put up a banner warning the crowd in Maltese and English of the illegality of the gathering and ordering them to disperse. If this failed, we fired tear gas, and finally, a single marksman would be ordered to shoot to kill an individual, who appeared to be the ringleader of the insurrection.

2. Our God appears to use a similar principle. As a loving Father, He longs for us to place Him first in our lives and obey His Commandments. In the Old Testament He would select certain patriarchs, priests or kings to stimulate the faith of His People (the Jews) in God. On being ignored, He would not give up but instead withdraw some of the blessings the people had become accustomed to in their settled existence by sending famines, earthquakes or plagues, as a wake-up call. Finally, if the people retained their stubborn resistance or lethargic attitude, He would leave them in the state they had adopted and no longer seek to 'soften' their hardened hearts. Therefore, even God has limits on His love because He presumably knows the danger of becoming like an over-indulgent father, who just lets his children get away with unruly and selfish behaviour: without an element of discipline, justice fails.

3. Consider God's use of the minimum force principal in Romans 1:18-24, *'The wrath of God is being revealed from heaven against all the godlessness and wickedness of men who suppress the truth by their wickedness, since what may be known about God is plain to them, because God has made it plain to them. For since the creation of the world God's invisible qualities – his eternal power and divine nature – have been clearly seen, being understood from what has been made, so that men are without excuse.*

4. *For although they knew God, they neither glorified him as God nor gave thanks to him, but their thinking became futile and their foolish hearts were darkened. Although they claimed to be wise, they became fools and exchanged the glory of the immortal God for images made to look like mortal man and birds and animals and reptiles. Therefore God gave them over in the sinful desires of their hearts to sexual impurity for the degrading of their bodies with one another.'*

5. In summary, as people choose to reject God, He allows them to do this by *'giving them over in the sinful desires of their hearts'* (Romans 1:24). This is really sad because there comes a time when even God gives up trying to call us to repentance and faith as He knows the effect of people's desire for independence from Him will result in their becoming slaves to whatever their rebellious nature has chosen. One can only imagine God's distress in turning away in dismay when He knows His loved ones, instead of choosing eternal life, have opted for spiritual death. Despite God moving from minimum through to maximum force, in offering eternal life to those who believe, when this appeal falls on 'deaf ears,' God respects our right to freedom of choice and eventually may give up appealing to us.

6. Covid is challenging because it reveals the fragility of life. In the Old Testament there are records of how God sent pestilences, usually to judge His people in the hope that they would repent and believe in Him. While Covid may be His method of judging apostasy in many parts of the world, it is also the outworking of His mercy: either He can leave people in their sin and condemnation, or, He can make a final attempt at drawing people away from slavery to selfishness, pride, addiction, power, status and avarice, by using Covid to try to bring people to their senses. As with the illustration of the military principle of 'minimum force,' God is providing one last chance to many intransigent people to avoid the final fatal option of, 'using the bullet,' resulting in spiritual death.

7. Many need to be shaken out of apathy to become aware of God. The Romans 1:18-24 passage (paragraphs 3 and 4 of this article) makes it clear that there is no excuse for not believing in God because He has revealed what He is like through His creation. Many take the attitude roughly summed up as, 'If there is a God, I have lived a good life so I will be all right when I die – I have never done anyone any harm.' Biblically, it is clear that this attitude would not qualify someone for eternal life. The first four of the Ten Commandments (Exodus 20:1-17) concern our attitude towards God – we should love Him and put Him first in our lives. Our subsequent service, filled with compassion and love to others, are covered in the last six commandments and should be an outworking of Christ's life in us. He summed up the purpose behind the Ten Commandments with these words (Matthew 7:12), *"So in everything, do to others what you would have them do to you, for this is the Law and the Prophets."*

8. We do not have the capacity within ourselves to keep these commandments because the Bible teaches that we are all sinners (Romans 3:23), *'All have sinned and fall short of the glory of God.'* Humanity inherited Adam's natural capacity to sin. God is holy and will not tolerate sin in His presence. In order to bring reconciliation between God and humanity, God sent His Son into the world to take our sinful nature and die with it in our place, so that we can recognize our condition and turn away from a sinful, selfish life. Having turned away from that life, we turn in faith towards Christ. This does not mean that we will never sin again, but it does mean that as we daily confess our sins in repentance to God, we will gradually learn that we are no longer slaves to sin and experience peace with God.

9. Man is composed of body, soul and spirit; it is with our spirit that we can communicate with God, who is Spirit. The Holy Spirit has an important role in bringing us into salvation. He 'tugs' at our spirit, as He did to members of a crowd of many thousands at Pentecost, while the apostle Peter was preaching (Acts 2:37), *'When the people heard* *this, they were cut to the heart and said to Peter and the other apostles, "Brothers what shall we do?"* Peter told them to repent, believe and be baptised.

10. The idea that after death we will just be put in a box and go into oblivion is clearly not regarded as the truth in the Bible. After death both believers and unbelievers will ultimately appear on Judgement Day before the Lord, Judge Jesus. This will happen after He returns in glory to the Mount of Olives, located just outside Jerusalem. Revelation 1:7 *'Look, he* (Jesus) *is coming with the clouds, and every eye will see him, even those who pierced him; and all the peoples of the earth will mourn because of him. So shall it be! Amen.'* The many who will mourn are those who suddenly realize that the coming of the Lord Jesus Christ means they are on the wrong side – at that stage it is too late to believe, as Jesus will appear before their eyes, ready to judge them.

How the Gospel influenced two national leaders
Chapter 3
King George VI – The Earth is the Lord's

1. '*The earth is the Lord's, and everything in it, the world, and all who live in it*' (Psalm 24:1).

Despite a powerful verse such as this, many in our society either hold God in contempt, or just ignore the possibility of His existence, as God can be seen as rather an outdated concept in our modern, civilized, technological era. The Bible is quite contemptuous of this atheistic attitude, dismissing it with these words in Psalm 14:1, '*The fool says in his heart, "There is no God."*'

2. Some may dimly remember from school days of the God of the Old Testament, who spent much time fighting for his beloved Jewish people. God certainly influenced battles in which the Jews were involved and continues doing this to this day, exerting His power in battles in accordance with His will. Psalm 24:8 states, '*The Lord strong and mighty, the Lord mighty in battle.*' One example was in the 'Miracle of Dunkirk,' which is well described in an internet article (see footnote).[2]

3. The main points of the article are that during the Second World War in May 1940 the British Expeditionary

---

[2] https://www.cufi.org.uk/opinion-analysis/the-miracle-of-dunkirk-when-a-nation-prayed/

Force was encircled by Rommel's armoured pincer movement. As the entire front was collapsing rapidly, it was decided to evacuate the troops through the port of Dunkirk. At the time Churchill believed only about 25,000 men would be successfully re-embarked: it seemed that much of the British Army would perish. In response to this tragic situation, King George VI requested that Sunday, 26th May, should be observed as a National Day of Prayer. He asked the people of Britain to commit their cause to God. Millions of people in all parts of the Commonwealth and Empire flocked to the churches to pray and God quickly responded with the following three miracles.

4. The first miracle was that for some reason Hitler overruled his generals and halted the advance of his armoured vehicles just ten miles away from annihilating the British Army. Churchill believed Hitler did this as he believed his air superiority would stop the evacuation.

5. The second miracle was linked to the first in that owing to appalling weather over Flanders, the German *Luftwaffe* squadrons were grounded. The bad weather allowed our Army to move to the coast in darkness. There have been instances when God intervened during battles using the weather and His creation to accomplish His plan. On one noticeable occasion (recorded in Joshua 10:12-13) while Joshua, a brave military leader of the Jewish people was fighting and overcoming his enemies, in order to 'finish his task,' he asked the Lord to make the sun stand still. This is what happened next, '*The sun stopped in the middle of the sky and delayed going down about a full day.*'

6. I gather that a few years ago when a complicated mathematical calculation had to be worked out for a space

project, the careful calculations kept coming up with the same figure, but always incorrect by some hours, until someone on the team remembered that the Bible recorded there was an occasion when the sun 'stood still' for a few hours; this recollection solved the mathematical problem – God provided an extra day at Joshua's request. The above passage continues (Joshua 10:14) *'There has never been a day like it before or since, a day when the Lord listened to a man. Surely the Lord was fighting for Israel!'* On 26th May 1940, the man the Lord listened to was the faithful King George VI, while the country the Lord fought for was Great Britain.

7. The third miracle, again revealed the hand of God, who controls the whole world, including its weather. Despite the storm over Flanders, a great calm, hardly ever previously experienced, settled over the English Channel and its waters were as still as a mill pond. This enabled a vast array of little and big ships to sail across to Dunkirk to bring back our stranded men; I assume that included my father, Brigadier Denison, who was in the British Expeditionary Force (although he never spoke to me about it).

8. The Lord was gracious to individuals 'on the ground.' A chaplain was machine-gunned and bombed as he lay on the beach. After a long time, he realized that he had not been hit, rose to his feet and found the sand around where he had been lying was pitted with bullet holes, and that his figure was outlined on the ground. In another incident, a group of 400 men were being bombed and machine-gunned systematically by about sixty enemy aircraft (which had managed to fly despite the bad weather):

the men were amazed that none of them were injured.

9. There were 335,000 men rescued from Dunkirk. As the prayers of the nation were answered, there was a Day of National Thanksgiving on 9th June 1940. Many of the church choirs sang the words of Psalm 124 which were felt to be apposite. One can imagine the feelings towards the Lord of relief and gratitude of the rescued soldiers and the brave mariners in their little boats, when they sang Psalm 124:6-8, *'Praise be to the Lord, who has not let us be torn by their teeth. We have escaped like a bird out of the fowler's snare; the snare has been broken, and we have escaped. Our help is in the name of the Lord, the Maker of heaven and earth.'*

10. It's important to acknowledge that the Lord is indeed the Maker of heaven and earth and everything in it. That is what millions of people did at the National Thanksgiving Day, giving praise and thanksgiving to God for the deliverance of the British Expeditionary Force as a result of the miracle at Dunkirk.

Chapter 4
Donald Trump – the day of small things?

1. Zechariah 4:10: *"Who despises the day of small things?"* The context of this verse is a minor prophet, called Zechariah, who received a vison from God during which these words were spoken to the prophet by an angel. Essentially, Zechariah was told to be content with small things rather than go for the 'big and beautiful.' It reminds us to be aware that what seems small and insignificant to us, may be highly regarded by God and instrumental to His plans.

2. It is often difficult for us to know what is important to God, but when seen in hindsight we can sometimes see His handiwork. Watching someone weave a tapestry, if seen from the rear of the tapestry looks like a jumble of wools, whereas on turning over the tapestry the full picture is apparent. Hindsight can be very illuminating! To illustrate how apparently unrelated events can turn out to be part of the Creator's plan, I am going to relate a real-life illustration. My information comes from articles on the internet. I have tried, as far as possible, to ascertain the truth of the facts.

3. The scene of the story is a windswept island, called Lewis, off the north coast of Scotland, with the following apparently unrelated events:-

1) There were few men living on the Island after the First World War, as many had been killed in the war. Sadly,

the situation was exacerbated after the end of hostilities when a ship bringing home soldiers and sailors to the Island sank a mile away from the Island, with the loss of 205 lives.

2) In 1930 one of the Islanders, Mary Ann MacCleod (aged seventeen years), youngest of ten children, decided that as there were so few eligible young men on the Island she would emigrate to the USA, where some of her sisters were already living. Year on year Mary would return to Lewis to the Presbyterian Church, where she had worshipped during her youth.

3) In 1949 the Hebridean Revival broke out on the Island. This was a powerful move of God through the Holy Spirit (the most recent significant revival in the UK); the main speaker was Rev Duncan Campbell. Many people on the Island were deeply affected by his challenging gospel messages.

4) Duncan Campbell was particularly grateful to two old women in their eighties (one blind and the other with a bad stoop), who prayed sometimes throughout the night for the revival meetings. There is a photo on the internet of Duncan arm in arm with these two prayer warriors.

4. After emigrating to the USA, Mary Ann MacCleod married Fred Trump and the couple had five children, the youngest being Donald Trump, who became the President. It would appear that Donald Trump was influenced by his mother's Christian experiences, as he visited one of the Lewes churches involved in the revival. While President, Donald Trump kept in the Oval Office a Bible that was used in a powerful way during the revival. I expect Donald was also influenced by the fact that the two old ladies praying for revival were his great aunts (see paragraph 3:4).

5. I make no comment on Donald Trump's conduct during his tenure as President, as it is the Lord who judges these things. Romans 14:4, '*Who are you to judge someone else's servant? To his own master he stands or falls. And he will stand, for the Lord is able to make him stand.*' However, I do use this story as an illustration of how, through God's subtle, intricate planning, arranging apparently unrelated events, He raises a person to high office. Psalm 75: 6-7 (King James Version): '*For promotion cometh neither from the east, nor from the west, nor from the south. But God is the judge: he putteth down one, and setteth up another.*'

6. We are told to pray for those in authority and also to acknowledge that they are so placed by the will of God. Colossians 1:15-16, '*He* (Christ) *is the image of the invisible God, the firstborn over all creation. For by him all things were created: things in heaven and on earth, visible and invisible, whether thrones or powers or authorities; all things were created by him and for him.*' The fact that all authorities are created by God and for him does not mean that the rulers and authorities will necessarily rule in accordance with God's righteous laws. That is a matter for the ruler concerned, who like all humanity, will have been blessed with freedom of choice; God seems to jealously guard freedom of choice as one of His important principles in life. After all, in the beginning Adam and Eve were given the choice whether or not to obey God in respect of eating from the 'Tree of Life.' Sadly, Adam and Eve made the wrong choice and we all reaped the disastrous consequences – even the Lord Jesus Christ, who, on our behalf had to suffer a horrible death on a cross in order to redeem fallen humanity by bringing forgiveness of sins to

those who repent. This offer of reconciliation with God is called 'salvation.'

7. You may well ask, "Do we really need salvation?" The Bible indicates God's answer is, "Yes, you do need salvation." Your response to that could be, "OK, but would it not be better to think about this when I have more time?" This second question is answered by Paul (2 Corinthians 6:2-3), in which he quotes God as follows, "*In the time of my favour I heard you, and in the day of salvation I helped you.*" *I tell you, now is the time of God's favour, <u>now is the day of salvation.</u>'*

8. We manage to fill our time with comparatively trivial, temporal things, which we believe are so much more important than our eternal destiny. God says that <u>now</u> is the day of salvation. Who knows if God will offer salvation again or whether we are suddenly taken ill with a deadly disease: if it is Covid, one is not in a fit state to think straight while straining for each breath – surviving on a ventilator. God is a realist, who knows that our 'heart' and attachments are all in this world. He loves us so much that He wants us to be freed from sin in Christ Jesus and offer us His favour and salvation. God's salvation does not mean that everything will be comfortable and easy for the rest of our lives. Sometimes, it is quite the reverse: it is estimated that there are currently 340 million Christians facing persecution. However, God is very close to us and in His love enables us to overcome all trials and difficulties through His grace and love.

How the gospel affected some sex offenders
Chapter 5
Setting up a Sex Offender Hostel

1. Stepping Stones Trust (SST) was a Christian charity providing support and accommodation to ex-offenders. I was the Chairman of SST during its entire existence of twenty-eight years. It closed in 2012, passing its accommodation and services to a larger Christian charity – at the time of SST's closure it had 'bed spaces' for seventy-four ex-prisoners. One of SST's smaller hostels was specifically designed for sex offenders – this hostel no longer exists. When I received an OBE for the work of SST, the Queen seemed particularly interested in our sex offender hostel. However, little did she know about the trials and tribulations we encountered in setting up and operating this hostel.

2. After opening our first Christian hostel for offenders, we received a number of requests from sex offenders for accommodation but were unable to accept these referrals, as sex offenders and ordinary offences 'do not mix.' This is why in prison sex offenders are normally segregated for their own protection, under what is known as 'Rule 43.'

3. Seeking to follow Christ's example of gravitating towards those 'on the margins of society,' we decided that we should open a small specially designated sex offender

hostel. As a probation officer I knew we were taking on a very difficult task. The trustees of SST were dedicated Christians, who recognized God's calling in this matter.

4. The SST trustees were aware that no landlord would be prepared to lease a hostel to accommodate sex offenders, therefore we had to raise sufficient capital in order to purchase a building for this purpose. Fundraising from the public to assist sex offenders would inevitably be a 'non-starter,' as it was hardly a popular cause. However, the Christian public 'caught the vision' and recognized this specific need, which we hoped might, in a small way, reduce some of the horrific sex offences. The trustees' first step was to 'test the water' in July 1997 by setting a fundraising target of £30,000, to be raised within three months. As the money was forthcoming, in October of the same year, we set a further target of £70,000 within seven months, which was also achieved – so with a total of £100,000 we purchased a hostel.

5. In the planning of this hostel, I was acutely aware of the experience of a Christian Probation Officer colleague, who, after retiring from the Probation Service, set up a charity to treat sex offenders and opened a specialized facility in the Midlands. He became an expert in this field and would comment on sex offender treatment in the national press and TV. Unfortunately, he became a 'victim of his own success' because he was recognized coming out of the sex offender facility, so the 'game was up' and there were later two arson attacks on the centre, which had to be closed. In view of his experience, the SST trustees were careful to take an 'anonymous route' to achieve our objective.

6. The location of the hostel was in an anonymous street. Anyone visiting the hostel was not allowed to park outside to avoid unnecessary attention. When a client was sentenced to a condition of residence at the hostel (which I will call 'x house'), the court were not allowed to mention the address in open court. The residents were told to be very careful about mentioning where they lived. Only police, probation, social services and medical and psychiatric services were allowed to know the address of 'x house.'

7. The local community did 'get wind' of the hostel, with the 'fire of protest' being fanned by the local press. I was not surprised at this response because on an earlier occasion, when trying to open a sex offender home in another London borough, there were seventeen critical articles in the local press against my proposal.

8. At 'x-house' we had to take precautions in case the public attacked the hostel residents, so we arranged with the local police for a quick emergency exit plan, should it be required. We also prayed that God would not allow the local residents to discover the location of our hostel. The Lord answered our prayers.

9. When we first applied to London Probation Service for approval for the hostel, we were told that they would neither approve it, nor provide a hostel liaison officer. Despite their response, we were blessed with so many referrals that after a few years they were prepared to appoint a liaison officer. I showed the local Assistant Chief Probation Officer around the hostel and she welcomed our work.

10. All our hostels were deliberately located near a church, prepared to offer suitable support to the residents.

In the case of 'x' house, the minister of the church was an SST trustee. He carefully planned how to broach the suggestion of his church welcoming sex offenders in their midst. It was a risky prospect as three quarters of his congregation of 400 members could be potential victims – women and children would be at risk as the hostel took both paedophiles and rapists. Over a period of four weeks at the Sunday morning and evening services, the minister warned the church of the intended link with the hostel. Only one member of the congregation complained about this suggestion.

11. Care had to be taken when deliberately allowing these offenders into the church. Each resident had to sign a contract, which laid down the twin requirements of the church and hostel. During residential church retreats the residents knew there would be someone assigned to watch their behaviour.

12. It is reasonable to presume that 'the proof of the pudding is in the eating.' After ten years in existence, the local police ran a check on every past and present resident at the hostel: none had been reconvicted for sex offences over that ten-year period. In total the hostel was in operation for eighteen years and during the whole of that time none of the residents were reconvicted for sex offences. Surely, this is a miracle and a testimony of the grace of God in all concerned, whether residents, staff, trustees, church members, professional staff and volunteers.

13. Psalm 68:6, '*God sets the lonely in families, he leads forth the prisoners with singing.*' On conviction sex offenders usually experience complete rejection by other prisoners, family, 'friends', as well as the general public.

They become extremely lonely and frustrated; in this state of mind they are more likely to re-offend. Being adopted into a church and hostel 'family' can give sex offenders encouragement to overcome their deviancy. This encourages a feeling of belonging, especially as the Lord *'leads them forth with singing.'*

14. Whilst I have related these events as if, through the Lord, I had been responsible for the remarkable things that happened in SST – in fact this was not the case. It was very much a team effort amongst fellow workers in the gospel; all involved were Christians. We had excellent CEOs, staff and trustees. I thoroughly enjoyed working with inspiring and dedicated trustees, especially Peter Flower, Lorna Windmill, Rev. Paul Perkin, Brian Greenaway, Tim Coales, Adesina Adesanya and also two now deceased trustees, Frank Simmonds and Lord Robertson of Oakridge.

Chapter 6
A poem advocating compassion for those on 'the margins of society.'

Please don't find fault with the man that limps
and stumbles along the road.
Unless you have worn the shoes he wears
or struggled beneath the load.
There may be tacks in his shoes that hurt
though hidden away from view,
or the bundles he bears, placed on your back,
would cause you to stumble too.
Don't find fault with the man who sins
or pelt him with words or stones,
Unless you are sure, yes double sure,
that you have no sins of your own.
You know perhaps, if the tempter's voice
should whisper as soft to you,
as it did to him when he went astray,
would cause you to stumble, too.
Don't laugh at the man who is down today
unless you have felt the blow
that caused his fall, or felt the shame
that only the fallen know.
You may be strong, but still the blow that once
was his, if dealt to you in the self-same way,
at the self-same time,
would cause you to stumble too.
Anon

Chapter 7
Introduction to Ex-Prisoners Testimonies

1. *'For it is by grace you have been saved, through faith'* (Ephesians 2:8). Faith, in this context, means confidence and commitment to God. Our faith is vital and well-pleasing to God, as through it we learn to completely trust and hope in Him as our 'resident boss.' The Bible describes faith as, *'being sure of what we hope for and certain of what we do not see.'* (Hebrews 11:1).

2. One of the best attested facts in history, substantiated by many eye witnesses, was Christ's sacrificial death and resurrection, providing us a way (through faith in Christ) to become reconciled to God. Therefore, God has provided humanity with facts to enable us to believe. However, because this happened over 2,000 years ago, sadly, many see this as irrelevant ancient history.

3. I believe that the nearest thing that we currently have as proof in the existence of God is the life changing effect that God has on 'saved' sinners – the most poignant examples being the massive changes quite often recognized in the lives of ex-prisoners. How does this happen? It is the Lord Jesus Christ, through the Holy Spirit, operating in people's hearts, minds and spirits. This was prophesied by Jeremiah about 2,600 years ago, when God said through the prophet, *'I will put my law in their minds and write it on their hearts, I will be their God, and they will be my people.'*

(Jeremiah 31:33).

4. In the testimonies that follow, notice the gradual, but quite substantial, changes in the attitudes and conduct of the men, as they become Christians: spiritually growing through the instruction and guidance of the Holy Spirit.

5. Working as a probation officer for thirty-seven years, I saw some positive changes in individual secular offenders. However, a Home Office Probation Inspector once told me that in his inspections he found that by far the most significant and lasting changes were in those who had become Christians; I agreed with him. I discovered that many Christian ex-prisoners did not need to be taught at any depth about moral issues, as the Holy Spirit made it clear to them (individually) what was expected in respect to loving God and their 'neighbours' – the essential issues of the Ten Commandments. In effect I saw Jeremiah's prophecy (see paragraph 3 above) being fulfilled in them – God put His law in their minds and wrote it in their hearts.

6. Bob Kimmerling, one of the former CEOs of SST, used the men's own words to compile the following testimonies from past residents who had stayed in SST's various accommodation units, which included flats, large and small hostels. Bob has given permission to publish these testimonies – the men's names have been changed. Bob is currently co-minister of the Vineyard Life Church in Richmond, Surrey. The church is involved in providing empowerment and other training courses for the homeless, as well as a Food Bank. For further information go to:- www.vineyardcommunity.org.uk

Chapter 8
A Sex Offender's Testimony

1. Many people believe that when someone is sent to prison it means they have lost their freedom. In reality it is much more than that. They can also lose their family, friends, income, work and colleagues. They lose their sense of pride and dignity, self-esteem, self confidence and trust of others.

2. Coming out of prison 'alone,' this seems an impossible task to overcome. To someone who has already lost these values the worst position would be to return to cope without support of others, or to feel that nobody genuinely cares about them. The 'easy' option is often to re-offend and it's a matter of time before they are back doing another sentence!

3. Offering an ex-offender a truly Christian home on release is to offer much more than accommodation. It actually gives them the opportunity to begin the process of rebuilding themselves; something which cannot be done as a 9 to 5 job and it does not happen overnight!

4. To have a home where people can re-value themselves and reflect on their circumstances which lead them to prison with a totally different and clearer point of view is what is needed to begin the rebuilding process. It is important that they can have others around them who genuinely care and who can act as role models, to be shown

that the change can be achieved and the difference it makes in their lives.

5. There is a need for the residents to feel fully accepted in the home and the community. By building up links with other Christians in the home and at the Church, feelings of rejection can be overcome. I feel that the support, encouragement and commitment that has been given to me in this area would just not be offered in the same way in a non-Christian household. If a Christian ex-offender is surrounded by non-Christians and their lifestyle and morals, then they can easily slide back into situations which would lead them to re-offending.

6. If ex-offenders are to be encouraged to change their thoughts, feelings and whole way of life and become responsible members of the community, then they need all the unconditional love and commitment that is given by fellow Christians. The most difficult part of any change is at the beginning and this is the time that most support is needed.

How the Gospel effected 'ordinary' offenders
Chapter 9
Alex

"I was brought up in a children's home in Ealing during the 1960s. I felt different at school because in those days I was the only darker face. I was affected by ill health and was always picked last in sports teams. I was also a very distant child and spent my time on my own, playing with my toy soldiers, with no experience of close relationships or intimacy.

"We all went to church at Ealing Abbey and it was there that I discovered God took up some people's thoughts and time but I just felt unworthy. Why would God bless a nobody like me? For me it made sense for God to reward good people but I was not good; my penitence was a mockery; I would confess, be asked to say a hundred 'Our Fathers,' and then do the same thing again.

"I left the children's home at 16 and stayed with my mum, whose boyfriend was a hard villain. I wanted to pretend to be hard like him so I used to take a knife to football matches. I got my first ten convictions just trying to prove I was one of the boys, but I was really a lonely person walking the streets of Brighton with nobody to talk to. I was at the bottom of the pit. If I had the courage, I would have topped myself. I thought I could die and no one would notice or be effected. I had to do something to get attention, to be listened to, and so I did my first robbery.

"When I was awaiting trial for the robbery offence, I felt like a machine inside the Criminal Justice System. Still, nobody seemed to want to know about me, or my life, or the reasons why I was there. Only three days before the robbery I had cried out to God, "If you are real, then show me."

"In Lewes prison I found some rest. I was being fed and I had a chance to be noticed in chapel. The attention was flattering and I fell in love with a Catholic visitor. I never thought that a woman of her class would want to say hello to the likes of me; I was so thin and underweight. I started to feel feelings that had been suppressed but I could not cope so I went to the Protestant chapel instead.

"The songs began to affect me. I was holding back the tears; I was beginning to think that maybe I could ask Jesus to have mercy on me and come into my life. I was given the chance on Good Friday in 1986. The Chaplain laid a cross on the floor and asked those who wanted Jesus to come and kiss it. He told us that doing this was symbolic but it was the act of faith that mattered.

"I took my turn and bent down and kissed the cross. I said sorry to Jesus and felt a shock go through my body. I felt the love and the pain of the cross, and at that moment I learnt that I meant something to God. I fell in love with Him and I had a great two and a half years in jail and I was rebuilt physically in the gym.

"I had not thought where I was going to go when I got out and I didn't get much help. On release I went to a hostel in Brighton but I had no idea about how to look after myself. I tried going to local churches but no one wanted to help me. I felt unwelcome and after a few days of putting my Bible on my bed and reading and praying, I started to get distracted. It wasn't long before I didn't hear God or speak to Him. I then met a very pretty woman and God 'went out the window' altogether.

"I could not cope and I was lonely and had deep areas of healing still to happen in my life. I did not feed myself very well or have any friends. I was lost and longed to be back in prison. It was less than three months before I ended back inside serving four years.

"At my next release I came to one of the SST's homes, where I stayed for nine months. This was a turning point for me. They gave me a safe place to live, lots of attention and introduced me to a welcoming church where I could worship and learn to be part of a family. I had never experienced human love before as I had spent a lot of time in a single cell where I had been stuffed full of drugs. I had to learn how to get on with people: simple things like agreeing what to watch on the telly, eating together and washing up.

"Without support I would have still been 'easy game' for Satan. A lifetime of hurt and rejection needs the daily experiences of God's love through fellowship with His people. I had this at the hostel and local link church, where I was slowly built up to learn what was OK, that I was worth loving, that I did have a hope and that some people on this planet of ours liked me. When I messed up I was just shown how to do better next time and forgiven. I was shown God's love in action."

Alex's recovery was long and difficult. After a number of jobs and some time at college, he returned to work at one of the SST hostels.

Chapter 10
Brian

Brian was living in a tent for five months, before coming to an SST hostel. During that time he successfully raised sponsorship for the Trust through running the London Marathon. He now hopes to attend Bible College. Following is his poem entitled, 'I ain't running':-

Got up this morning
to say our prayers
Jasper came in
"Police downstairs"
I looked through the window
what did I see!
Old Bill's car
THEY'VE COME FOR ME!
They've come for me
but I ain't running
I've found a place
to face what's coming
I've found strength from
the girl I love
my brothers here
my family there
Our Father above.
Footsteps on the stairs
Drawing near
Last chance to get out of here

but I'm holding
face to face with the nasties
in my place
nearly folding
IS IT ME

Chapter 11
Colin

"I've lived down South all my life, we used to live in an old prefab but ended up a road where my family have been for about 25 years. We had a lot of arguments and I rebelled a bit. My dad didn't want a son – I've got three sisters – and I got into trouble when I was only eight. As soon as I was old enough I went to juvenile court but before that my mum used to march me back to shops to apologise for nicking sweets. As I got older I got into bad company. So much was happening at home. My dad was a long-distance lorry driver and used to have arguments with mum about me when he came home. My mum worked in a bottle factory. We didn't see much of either of them. The baby sitters used to say to mum, 'we'll look after your three daughters but we're not looking after him again.' One of them would hold my face down under the bath, which made me even more difficult to deal with.

"My parents bought me a tape recorder one year but I broke into a school and stole a much better one. They said, 'why did you want that when we bought this one?' I was insecure and didn't feel that I was wanted anyway. I wanted some love, not gifts. My mum couldn't handle me any longer and when I was aged thirteen they put me on a five year Care Order with Social Services. As things got worse, I went to borstals and on to prison.

"In 1983 a new family moved in. They used to have

wild parties; all sorts went on. First off they thought my mum was being nosy. She was always at the window and they thought she was going to tell the Social about them. They didn't know she was having breathing problems. This family called her names and things but I became friends with them and used to go into their house, which she didn't like.

"Later on, though, these lads used to come round nearly every night throwing bricks and things. We'd call the police but they said they couldn't do anything. They would look at my dad's broken windscreen and just laugh. We gave them names but they weren't interested. The lads used to come from a nightclub, sometimes three and four o'clock in the morning, putting bricks through bedrooms, living rooms, anywhere they wanted. Mum had the grandchildren staying. I was living with one of my sisters at the time but it got so bad that I went back and slept on the settee. One night they put a light to dad's van but because it was diesel it didn't go up, that's how serious things were getting. They would phone up with taunts like 'nice windscreen on your dad's van,' and so on.

"They came again on January 13th at half past midnight and lobbed bricks through the front door. Mum said, 'oh no, not again.' Dad jumped out of his chair and took a pickaxe handle. I thought, 'should I go running after dad or stay with mum?' They both had bad medical conditions so I didn't know who to protect. In the end I told mum to phone the police and ran after dad. I found him round the corner on his knees. He was hysterical, shouting for someone to stop them, but no one was interested.

"I just snapped. I grabbed his axe handle and chased

after one of the lads. He was giving me the 'come-on' as I was chasing him. I didn't know he was trying to lure me to his mates down the road.

"When I caught up I just hit him once with the handle and right after I hit him the police came round the corner. If I had seen them a couple of seconds earlier I probably wouldn't have done it but I was wound up so much that I just couldn't stop myself.

"The police stopped and saw the lad on the ground. I said, 'I did it, I'm not going anywhere,' and I just got into the police car by myself. I was being driven back to the station and they had the radio on. They didn't have a chance to turn the volume down before it came over that he had suffered a cardiac arrest. He had been drinking alcohol and had 235 milligrams in his bloodstream so they couldn't give him any drugs. They did what they could. I didn't hit him hard but where I had hit him was a vulnerable spot and the drink had relaxed his muscles so he had haemorrhaged.

"When I heard he had died I was shocked. I didn't say anything for a long time. I was in tears. I just admitted that it was my fault and not my dad's. The people against my dad tried to say it was him as well and the police said we had both gone off with pick axe handles but later they had to admit that was not right.

"Because of the threats my dad was arrested, supposedly for his own protection. He was in Winchester Prison with me. We thought that he was going to be put in a hospital because he wasn't well but every time the case came to court, the victim's mates were there. We thought he would only be in prison for a couple of weeks but he ended up spending 15 months inside before he was acquitted. He was pretty bitter about that: even the prosecution said that he had done nothing.

"I received seven years for manslaughter with provocation, which was reduced to 4 years on the grounds of diminished responsibility. But I was so low in prison and on antidepressants. As far as I was concerned, I had taken someone's life and I wanted to take my own. I didn't understand the difference between manslaughter and murder and for the 15 months before my trial, before I got a decent QC, I really thought I was going to be locked up for life. I knew I couldn't handle being banged up in a little box for all that time.

"A couple of days before the trial I was talking to a chaplain. They knew I was at risk and I was telling him how I thought life wasn't worth living. He was telling me that Jesus loves me and that my sins would be forgiven if I repented. I prayed a prayer and when I looked up at the window, suddenly the cell became filled with light. He saw it as well. It was like the sun passed over, backwards and forwards, waving. I thought I was cracking up – really cracking up, but I felt so good inside, like all the weight was being lifted off my shoulders. I had a new confidence that day.

"I went to the chapel that afternoon and I was shouting my head off, I've never felt anything like it. I got so full of confidence. I remember this group came in one day and nobody clapped when they finished, so I started clapping and told the others to give them some encouragement. I never would have done that before. So many miracles have happened. When I was in prison, I had a cyst on my head the size of a boiled egg but a friend that I met in

Wandsworth Prison put her hands on it and prayed and it went. The prison officers and people who used to make jokes couldn't believe it.

"When I got back from the Appeal Court they gave me my parole papers straight away because I was already one month into parole. I had been going regularly to the chapel and Bible studies: there were lots of Bible studies in Winchester Prison but in Wandsworth Prison many of the studies were cancelled. I spent the second half of my sentence in Wandsworth Prison. They didn't think I would get parole so they weren't prepared with a release plan but the chaplain said she knew about 'Stepping Stones.' When they came up with a place in Bournemouth, I said it was too late as I already had a place to go to. It was dangerous for me to go back to my home area.

"I think my hurts and rejections are still there a little bit but the Lord is working on them and I can never deny what God has done for me. I just wish I'd become a Christian sooner."

Chapter 12
Dennis

Early days

I was born and brought up in Zimbabwe in a Christian family, where my mother, brothers and sisters were much more devout than my father. To begin with, I was never interested in going to church, although I went with my family to the Seventh Day Adventist Church.

As my father liked to approach the big questions of life in a scientific way, he was not really attracted to Christianity, and so, influenced by him, neither was I. When I went to the High School, I felt confused because I was attending both Bible lessons and also Science lessons. There was an obvious conflict between them, and I believed far more in Science than in the Bible.

Starting work in the army

When I went on to join the army, I learned to believe and trust in myself and in what I was trained to do. I felt that people calling themselves Christians had never suffered hardship at this particular time in Zimbabwe's history. It was not until I was in the war front in the Democratic Republic of Congo that I experienced the transforming difference in life between non-believers and believers in Jesus Christ; they committed themselves to pray and acknowledge the hardships that they faced.

As time went on, I was drawn by these Christians both to listen to God and find His Peace. It was extraordinary to me that they could believe in someone without having actually seen Him. I joined in with them, but without any proper understanding or faith. However, how they prayed for their families, including everyone in the group, did move me very deeply. I was also touched by how they prayed for other people, who were not in their position, and who were suffering from sickness or difficulties in different parts of the world.

Gradually the goodness of their perspective on life, as well as their evident gift in bringing peace to their colleagues, dawned on me. But I also felt let down by them because they never demonstrated any love to the civilian people living around them. When I pointed out this discrepancy in their behaviour, I was reprimanded as being more of a politician than a soldier. That lack of consistency worried me. It led me to be treated very differently, because my fellow soldiers were concerned about this so-called political influence. Seeing the civilian people dying all around me, including the terrible atrocities committed against them, struck me as grossly unfair.

Leaving the army and fleeing to England

When my leave fell due, I decided not to return to the war front. I left the Congo and escaped to the UK on a flight in August 1999. As soon as I arrived, on a Saturday morning, I applied for political asylum to the Immigration Authorities here. For the first six months in London, I didn't want to associate myself with Christian believers. Having no interest in going to church, since I felt terribly let down and thought that all Christians would be like the ones I had left behind in the army, very hypocritical.

Life in London

Now living in London, a stranger overheard me talking on my mobile phone in the street. She was called Justine. She thought I was Zimbabwean, but grew confused hearing me talk in a South African language (I am in fact half Zimbabwean, half South African). After we had talked together for a little while, Justine invited me to come to church with her, as she herself came from South Africa. As we 'ticked' along well, I agreed to go with her to her local Pentecostal church in Stratford, East London.

The first few weeks proved quite strange, as this was a new type of worship for me. I found it hard making friends with the members of the congregation. It was a very small church, but very noisy, with a lot of shouting all over the place, very full of the Holy Spirit. Many people were speaking incomprehensibly, but this I later discovered to be called, 'speaking in tongues'.

After a while, I disassociated myself from this church because as an asylum seeker, I was growing increasingly depressed. The Home Office wrote to say that they had turned down my application to stay, even though I already had a job as a security guard. I felt extraordinarily lonely and dejected. The Home Office kept me in their holding office for eleven days, and when I came out, I had lost both my flat and job.

Funds were running low. Although I started looking for new work, I got myself into bad company and ended up committing a crime, being charged with conspiracy to steal. In court, I justified this crime as my effort to try and make ends meet in order to pay the rent owing on my flat. The whole situation proved very tough.

In prison

I went to prison in December last year and was sentenced to four months imprisonment. I don't know why but after all the turmoil leading up to this crime, and then the court sentence, from my first day in prison until my last, I found life 'inside' very peaceful. I felt so much better in my head. My first day in prison coincided with the start of an Alpha Course. I had no idea what this was but discovered it included lively discussions on Christianity. Different denominations were involved from different churches. We had the opportunity to ask what Christianity was all about. I started to understand and believe. People of many different denominations were taking part in the course yet they all had a firm belief in Christ Jesus.

I saw I was making wrong judgements and choices in my life; mixing with wrong people; receiving wrong information both in books that I was reading and from programmes on television. I realised that I was choosing to be depressed and putting myself in difficult situations.

Politics has always been one of my great passions, and I have read many political books. These have made me quite depressed, although I never quite knew why. By being with Christians on the Alpha Course and asking a lot of questions, I learned to take the first steps towards trying to lead a better life. Depression free and loving the people around me, this was all new to me! In the past I had always kept myself to myself. I finished the Alpha Course which lasted ten weeks.

Commitment to Jesus

Someone from Holy Trinity Church in Brompton visited High Point Prison in May 2002. While she was teaching, I had a strong vision that there was no way I could continue living my previous life, so I made a commitment that day to follow Jesus Christ. From that day to this, I have continued to believe in Jesus Christ without any of the past doubts which used to trouble me so. The Prison Chaplain really helped me in answering my questions, and more especially in strengthening my faith.

I asked him to try to find me a church before my release date. He very kindly found me a college in which I could study theology, but unfortunately, I was not entitled to any benefits so I couldn't qualify for a college place.

The way forward

I also asked for help with accommodation and the Prison Chaplain contacted a Trust called 'Stepping Stones.' It was looking for people who had completed the Alpha Course in prison and were interested in living with other Christians. I was very pleased to find somewhere, where as a non-smoker and non-drinker, I could live with other Christians and look to strengthen my faith in Christ Jesus. I was delighted by the staff who could be role models and help us to improve our faith, to know Jesus much better and to study the Bible; I was accepted for a place at Park View, although in fact I moved on quite quickly to another of their hostels in Croydon. Since that first day, my faith in God has been tremendous. I no longer worry about the things I used to. I wake every morning giving my day to Jesus and we have Devotions after breakfast, which really uplifts me. I now accept every sort of person – completely different from my past life. The Ichthus summer holiday at Ashburnham with staff and other residents proved a particular blessing. It is a great and good experience to find a real focus for my life and I give enormous thanks to Stepping Stones.

Postscript

The Home Office decided that my appeal to remain in the UK should be approved in September last year. In God's grace, I have been able to secure a proper job. I also have found a decent place to live where I have a strong supportive church nearby with excellent teaching and a great congregation.

I am delighted that I have been able to enrol at the Open University to study for an Honours degree in Social Sciences, which I hope to complete in December 2005. It is quite tough juggling my academic studies with a full-time job but God renews my strength every day.

I have been given a vision by God to move forward to help others who have been in the same predicament as myself, because I will be able to identify clearly with the challenges that face them. My local home group is very encouraging and its members are working with me to bring this vision to fruition. Praise God.

Chapter 13
Ernest

Ernest came to Stepping Stones early in 2000 after being deported from America. At the time we had three deportees, another American and an Australian. They all went through very hard times with the unexpected separation from family and friends after prison release and ending up in an unfamiliar country. Ernest tells his own story of the events that led up to his new life.

"I was born in Birmingham and moved to the States when I was a kid, a place called Leftrak City. It was kinda hard when I got there. You just knew it wasn't right to be alone. I was scared but it didn't take me long to adapt. I met a few home boys and joined a gang called the 'Bloods,' the 57th Avenue Bloods.

"How you join the Bloods is you get beaten in by running a line with guys either side taking blows at you. I made it through there, had my palm cut and made a blood pact, blood in and out. They were great guys and we had a lot of fun. We sold drugs on the corner, cocaine and did drive-bys. We protected our territory and anybody who came into our neighbourhood trying to get what we had would have problems. It was like a family and we cared about each other and what we thought, but it was all violence and destruction, not a true family. I hung around them for a while and got into a few problems robbing stores.

"I robbed my first store at sixteen. It was the scary time

of my life. I grabbed this lady by the throat, got the money and ended up in Manhattan. When I called home my mom already knew about it. The police were looking for me and were asking a lot of people where I was, not just me but my friend also. Up to this day I never got taken for this crime, somehow, I escaped and stayed in New York, Brooklyn, and started hanging around a Jamaican gang, called 'Possy.' I met a young dread and started selling weed and crack cocaine. I saw there was a lot of money to be made out of that and people with smart cars, gold chains, beautiful women on each arm and all that, and I wanted it.

"I think I got that when I moved to California, near the Mexican border. It was just ripe for the 'picking.' I was making so much money and had joined the Lincoln Park 1904 Bloods. My home boy was an O.G., an old gangster, a one-time pimp and hustler. He took me under his wing and taught me a lot of things and introduced me to major movers and shakers. That's when I met a friend called 'Hose,' who sold drugs over the Mexican border. Everyone knew Hose. He had about ten runners and I wanted to make it like that too and I had my runners too. I knew that no one would try to front me and take what was mine and I did this for about seven months.

"I got into fights, got stabbed, shot, thrown out of windows. But the scariest thing was I enjoyed my life and I didn't care what happened. I went out busting and capping, shooting people if they got in my way. I had this friend Peewee. He said I was a demented person, not caring, not feeling. I didn't have time to feel I was making money. If I wanted it I just took it – I was just taking my slice of American pie.

"I had been to county jail before and that was nothing but then I went to the Penitentiary. That just sealed it all. It gave me time to reflect, and a downward spiral. They sent me to Donovan State Pen. I was shaking, not knowing what to expect and you hear all these stories about the Pen. I saw a couple of my home boys there and I saw this big sign on the wall saying, 'Warning shots will not be given.' There was this guy with an M16, or some high-powered rifle, I looked at him and this cold chill went through me. I swore and thought 'man, what am I doing.' We were locked up 23 hours a day. I had a lot of time to think. I had been caged and it was hard. Being locked up, I met a few guys from my neighbourhood and hung out. I met a lot of guys doing 15, 20 years and 45 years to life. I thought, 'man, thank God I'm not doing time like that.' But I was stuck in my head, I was naïve and I was a hard ass and they transferred me from Chuckawalla in the Mojave Desert.

"My cellmate was Evan, a young gangbanger from LA who used to preach at me and read the Bible out loud and I'd think 'oh man, he's reading the Bible again' and I would leave. It was like an everyday thing and sometimes he'd ask difficult questions; 'Do you believe in the Holy Spirit? Do you believe in Jesus?' I grew up a Roman Catholic but I was never a practising Christian but my mum was a Christian, goes to church all the time: I hurt her a lot but this was not me. I thought that people who come in the Pen and get into a jam, all of a sudden they turn to God, but when they get out of that sticky situation they're back to their old ways, so figured it was a fake.

"It was hard. I didn't even have the courage to talk to my mom or write her a letter. I just couldn't stand that call, me saying, 'I'm in a state prison' and her picking up and hearing me. I know I've disappointed her a great deal, it's not what any mother wants for her son. I thought I knew everything, that I was tough but I wasn't. I wasn't as strong as I thought I was. Jail can break a person down and I had nowhere else to turn but to God.

"Immigration came to see me. At that time they asked me where was I born. I tried lying and said, 'New York,' but two weeks later they came back and said, 'No, no, you were born in England.' At that point I still thought I was getting out and I'd be back on the streets, seeing my girl and all that stuff. It got down to 45 days and they took me out of Chuckawalla and sent me to Santonella State prison. It was back to the same thing just like Donovan, locked up 23 hours a day. They let me out one day and Immigration came to see me asking more questions. When I got back to my cell I thought to myself, 'What's going on here?'

"At Santonella I knew nobody. All I had was my Bible and some materials from the pastor. I would write little phrases on the wall and stuff like that. When you walk into a cell you also see little phrases on the wall that help guys do their time, something inspiring. I always came back to John 3. Nicodemus saying, 'How can a man be born again?' For some reason I always came back to that, him asking those questions of Jesus, and I suppose I felt like him, asking those questions too.

"I had always been alone. I had my family but I felt truly alone inside, you know what I mean? The only thing was contact with the Bible. I could get lost in it. Then they transferred me from C to D wing and I was able to get outside a little longer every day and I would sit on the benches near these guys, who were having a Bible study. I would sit there and listen, not joining in, but just listening a little way off to the side. There was this one guy, and you meet some truly gifted people in the penitentiary, I would swear he was a pastor. The stuff he was coming out with was spell binding. You know he felt it, there was something inside him that was different, but I was always just too scared. It was just like when you want to go to church. You know you want to go but you're too scared.

"I never asked them anything, I just kinda sat there and listened to what they were saying and I felt a little lifted but at the same time I was not sure what was happening because Immigration weren't telling me anything and I didn't know if I was getting out. I read my Bible and kept myself to myself. They had me in a cell with a guy named, 'Bear.' He was just a gruesome, nasty man, a real big guy and me and him just didn't get on. When my 45 days were up they sent me to Imperial Valley, a detention centre where they hold immigration guys. I had problems with the County Officers (Prison Officers), It seems like whenever I went to a different place there were always one or two C.O.s who had a hard on for me because of my size and wanted to chop me down.

"I was having problems but I was searching, but the main reason I gave my life over to God was when they put me on the plane, I went to the bathroom and just cried. The person was knocking on the door and I was like, 'I'll be there in a minute.' I cried. I had lost everything that day. I lost my girl, I lost my family, everything. I said, 'OK God, I give up.' I got off that plane and didn't know where I was or what I was going to do – I was terrified.

"I prayed. I was seriously, seriously praying and I got down on my knees and asked for forgiveness. I do that a lot more now, and in a way, I feel as if I'm coming into my own. A lot of things happened, finding Stepping Stones, helping me get on my feet and putting me on firm ground with the Bible, and a family love that is more genuine than the support of a gang. I see a lot of changes happening in me, more so today than when I was in the States.

"One of the things about being in the gang is that you show no emotions, no feelings at all. Now God is breaking me down. Some days I bawl like a baby, uncontrollably, but I know 'a humble and contrite spirit He does not despise.' I've come a long way, I know I have, but I know I've still a long way to go. I've wasted a lot of years but I'm learning to forgive myself like Jesus has forgiven me."

Chapter 14
Fred

"I appeared for trial at Snaresbrook Crown Court for supplying a class 'A' drug and if found guilty was looking at a probable sentence of between 14 and 16 years. Before the start of the trial, I said to the judge, 'Your honour, I want to change my plea from not guilty to guilty.' The court was absolutely packed and he said, 'I beg your pardon.' I said, 'I want to change my plea from not guilty to guilty, and I want my barrister to ask me all the questions he asked me yesterday because I think I unwittingly told some lies.' He said to me, 'Are you feeling all right?' and I said, 'Yes sir.' I'm not looking at him, he's right there, but I'm looking ahead and the prosecutor stood up and I know he's just sitting there like a lion on a doe, and I know he's got me. Then the judge said to me, 'Why do you want to change your plea?' 'Well,' I said, 'I've come to the conclusion, your honour, that I can't relate to the criminal brain that I had when all these events happened because I am no longer the same person.'

"I'm looking ahead, I'm not looking at him and I can't comprehend what's really happening. It's the Holy Spirit working but I'm not understanding this at the time, you see, it's just how I feel. The prosecutor comes up and says that we haven't got time for all this and I say, 'Your honour, this guy here is on about time and I've been stuck in a cell for thirteen and a half months, twenty-three hours a day, not knowing why I was there.' So, today, if you will accept my plea of guilty and the screw (prison officer) takes me back to my cell and locks the door, I will know why I'm there.' 'Well,' the judge says, 'Can you be explicit as to why you want to change your plea?' 'Yes, your honour, I want to change my plea because I have sinned against almighty God, who is my Father in heaven, and against my fellow man.' And he says to me, 'Are you sure you're all right?' And I said, 'I can assure you that I have never felt better in my entire life.' And all the court went, 'ooooh!' and they recessed for twenty minutes.

"Apparently, the confession was so sincere they actually thought I was going to die! They thought it was a last rite thing so when they came back, the judge says to me that he'll accept my plea providing I will see a doctor. I said, 'That's OK, that's fine by me.' So they sent me back to the cell and accepted my plea.

"The doctor came. It must have cost them a fortune, this big doctor from Harley Street. He says, 'Well, you've only got indigestion.' I said, 'I could have told you that before you got your stethoscope out of the bag.'

"So that was it. In the end I got five years. I was shipped to Wandsworth prison and told this Catholic priest what went on and he looked at me as if I was mad. He had an assistant chaplain who came down over a couple of weeks taking notes. He's sitting at one end of the table and I'm at the other end telling him everything and he's looking at my eyes all the time as if to see if there was any flaw in my story. He wasn't listening to me; he was thinking he'd heard all this before – another one who's trying for parole.

"But the Lord is so gracious because when it comes to

vetting, a woman comes and vets me and says she's going to recommend an open prison. This is unheard of: they were really strict about supplying class 'A' drugs in the 1990's, really heavy. One poor lad got five years for an eighth of a gram of cocaine and I got only five years for half a kilo. She came back and said, 'Upstairs they're not having it, but I'm adamant you're going to an open prison.'

"Three weeks after I came out of court, I picked my Bible up. It was I Timothy 6:12, *'Fight the good fight of the faith. Take hold of eternal life to which you were called when you made your good confession in the presence of many witnesses.'* Those words just came straight from my mind to my heart and they've stuck with me ever since.

"They never did believe me in Wandsworth but I wasn't bothered, I wasn't going to let anything deter me from my walk with the Lord. I started to get confused in Wandsworth because I couldn't understand what God was doing in my life, and the priest or chaplain thought I was working a scam. They simply didn't believe me. Worries about my family were concerning me and the Word of God gave me comfort, particularly Isaiah 28:16, *'So this is what the Sovereign Lord says: "See, I lay a stone in Zion, a tested cornerstone for a sure foundation; the one who trusts will never be dismayed."* I knew that the Lord was telling me to trust in Jesus.

"Then lo and behold they sent me to Stamford open prison. I sat down and talked with the chaplain and he listened to what I had to say about my experiences and I knew that he believed me.

"One day when I felt I couldn't go on with this God thing it suddenly dawned on me that if He was real, He could tell me Himself. I asked God to confirm what He had said to me on September 16th 1992 and sure enough God spoke to me through John 8:47, *'He who belongs to God hears what God says. The reason you do not hear is that you do not belong to God.'* In other words, he who comes to God hears God's words.

"That Sunday a group of Christians came to prison to minister to us all. They made an altar call and I responded and gave my life to Jesus. I knew my search was over. I heard the gospel and believed.

"But there was still something missing and still some confusion. I went to church, listening to all the visiting Christians and all that the Lord was doing for them and I felt gutted. One night I said to this bloke next to me, 'You Christians make me feel sick. You come in here saying that the Lord is doing this and that in your lives and I'm reading and studying the Bible every day and leading a good life in here but nothing like that is happening to me!' He then asked me if I was baptised in the Holy Spirit and I told him that I hadn't a clue what he was talking about. He showed me the scriptures from Acts 1:4-5, which is where Jesus said, *"Do not leave Jerusalem, but wait for the gift my Father promised, which you have heard me speak about. For John baptised with water, but in a few days you will be baptised with the Holy Spirit."*

"I asked if I could be baptised in the Holy Spirit. He prayed and nothing happened. He then put his hand on the back of my head and started praying in a language I had never heard before and almost immediately a great peace and joy came to me. I have never experienced anything so beautiful in my entire lifetime. I was so full of the Holy

Spirit and for four days I was on a high that nothing on earth could give me. I knew it wasn't a trip. I now know that God doesn't give you a trip but that He takes you on a journey. I got my parole on the due date and was released on February 20th 1994. I had met this someone in prison who had given his life to the Lord, or so we thought, so when I got out of prison I went to live with his mother and work in his business.

"There were certain conditions to this work, however, when I wouldn't compromise the Lord's way of doing things I was out on my ear after about six weeks.

"Thankfully, the chaplain at Stamford Hill Prison, phoned me up and said, 'I've got a place for you to stay at a Stepping Stones Trust hostel. I went up there and had the interview with the manager and after a week I moved in. I have to say that that was a rescue from the Lord because I don't really know what would have happened if it hadn't been for that place at Stepping Stones.

"That was a place where I had some big decisions to make. The drink had to go. I didn't have a problem I'd had in the past but I was drinking and I knew that had to go. I knew I had to take stock. I knew I had to seek the Lord and I knew I really had to study God's Word because the first thing that happened to me when I went to Stepping Stones was that there was a verse of scripture on the wall, Psalm 32:8, *'I will instruct you and teach you in the way you should go; I will counsel you and watch over you.'*

"The Lord has done that from that day to this, and I have to say that Stepping Stones gave me somewhere to take stock and really focus on what I wanted my future to be. I couldn't go where the criminal goes, although I knew hundreds of them, I couldn't go back to the old ground, back to my past, I had to go through this and decide what I'm going to do with my walk with the Lord, otherwise I'm back on the street, thieving, meeting up with criminals, back on the drink.

"With that stay at Stepping Stones, and the move of the Lord in my life, it gave me time to pursue what abilities I had for work and ministry and how to carry on walking with the Lord. Without it I don't really know what would have happened but I imagine it would have been back to the old ways with nobody to turn to."

Conclusion

These testimonies demonstrate how Jesus currently continues to reveal His 'special relationship' with the outcasts of society. At the start of His earthly ministry, He clearly identified (Luke 4:18 – 19) four categories of people to whom He was drawn (underlined), *"The Spirit of the Lord is on me, because he has anointed me to preach good news to the poor. He has sent me to proclaim freedom for the prisoners and recovery of sight to the blind, to release the oppressed, to proclaim the year of the Lord's favour."* Most prisoners fall within these categories, being poor, spiritually blind and oppressed.

Jesus did not enter paradise with one of His beloved apostles but with a repentant ex-offender, who was being crucified alongside Him. Jesus encouraged the ex-offender with these words (Luke 23:43), *"I tell you the truth, today you will be with me in paradise."*